SCHIRMER PERFORMANCE EDITIONS

CHOPIN

T0082077

SELECTED PRELUDES

Lower Intermediate to Intermediate Level

Edited and Recorded by Brian Ganz

To access companion recorded performances online, visit:
www.halleonard.com/mylibrary

Enter Code
3714-2318-7202-3657

Also available:
Chopin: Preludes (complete)
Edited and Recorded by Brian Ganz
Schirmer Performance Editions
HL00296523

On the cover:
The Composer Chopin Playing in the Salon of Prince Radziville in Berlin in 1829 (detail)

by Henry Siemiradzki
(ca. 1887)

© The Bridgeman Art Library/Getty Images

ISBN 978-1-4234-5523-3

G. SCHIRMER, Inc.

DISTRIBUTED BY
HAL•LEONARD®
CORPORATION
7777 W. BLUEMOUND RD. P.O. BOX 13819 MILWAUKEE, WI 53213

www.musicsalesclassical.com
www.halleonard.com

CONTENTS

HISTORICAL NOTES

FRÉDÉRIC FRANÇOIS CHOPIN (1810-1849)

Chopin was a pivotal figure in the history of the piano. He wrote music ideally suited to the "new" piano that was evolving during his life. As a result of developments in piano technology, the new instruments were capable of producing a broader palate of colors than their predecessors. They also allowed pianists to execute much faster, more intricate, delicate passage work than earlier instruments. Chopin used these elements of the new instruments, along with the sound-altering capabilities of the instrument's *una corda* pedal, to create music full of subtly interwoven melodies and colorful, modal harmonies. He established the piano as a solo instrument, performing his own fluid, expressive music with a delicate touch and tremendous sensitivity. Virtually all of his compositions were either pieces for solo piano or pieces that featured the piano prominently.

Born near Warsaw, Poland, to a Polish mother and a French father, Chopin was an undeniable prodigy. The boy's precocious playing opened the doors of Warsaw salons, where he quickly became the darling of society, and reveled in the elegance and style of that world. Chopin began writing music as a child as well, publishing his first pieces at age seven. Following his education at the Warsaw Conservatory, he left Poland for Vienna in 1830 to make a name for himself in the cultural capital. But he eventually settled in Paris, where he became a sought-after teacher and, once again, a favorite performer in the salons of the wealthy and aristocratic, where educated, cultured people gathered to hear the latest music, poetry, or literature of the day.

Famous for his fussy, fashionable clothing and handsome face, Chopin led a pampered life. A small, frail man weighing just over 100 pounds, he was quite sensitive about his physical stature because he felt it kept him from making as big a sound on the piano as he, and his critics, would have liked. Accordingly, Chopin enjoyed playing in the small salons, or drawing rooms, of wealthy music lovers. He felt these spaces were suited to his relatively small sound and they did not cause him the nervous tension he felt when playing in large halls. In fact, Chopin's legendary reputation as a performer stems from a total of about 30 public, concert-hall performances over the course of his entire career. Chopin preferred to be known as a composer, a reputation Robert Schumann helped build by writing, in a review of Chopin's *Variations*, Op. 2, "Hats off, gentlemen, a genius!"

Chopin was never able to return to Poland, due to political upheaval and war there, and he always missed his homeland deeply. He incorporated some of the folk music he heard as a youth into lovely, longing pieces of music. Although he never married, Chopin carried on a nearly decade-long affair with the bold novelist George Sand (Aurore Dudevant). She lived a wildly bohemian, outspoken lifestyle, smoking cigars and dressing in men's clothing. But she became a tender, maternal care-giver to the composer, creating the happiest, most productive period of his life. Chopin's frail health, diminished by tuberculosis, deteriorated during their years together, plummeting after their break-up. He died two years later, at age 39, and was buried in Paris. Mozart's *Requiem* was performed at his funeral, which was attended by almost 3,000 people.

—*Elaine Schmidt*

PERFORMANCE NOTES

Some General Comments

The *Preludes* of Frédéric Chopin are among the most beloved works in all of piano literature, and among the most often studied and performed. In no other works is Chopin's genius for brevity and poetry on more vivid display. In no other works are there such varied levels of difficulty, offering gratification to the near beginner as well as challenge to the seasoned professional. And in no other works does Chopin explore as large or as satisfying a range of emotional states.

But although the *Preludes'* nearly universal affection and widespread familiarity are well deserved, they come with a price. For sometimes a piece we hear frequently becomes harder and harder to hear truly. It is as if a kind of cellophane or plastic wrap begins to grow around the music, and listening to it can be like eating food we have forgotten to remove from its packaging. If a piece reaches this stage in our experience, we are likely to say it has grown stale and put it aside for a while, perhaps for good. But what if there were a way to tear off the cellophane and interact with the piece with both the skill born of familiarity and the thrill of first-time discovery?

In this edition of the Chopin *Preludes* I have endeavored to offer the pianist tools for removing the cellophane from these much loved and familiar pieces and discovering their originality anew. Although I have taken a "less is more" approach to the score itself, seeking to preserve a relatively direct contact between composer and performer, I have sought in the performance notes to share insights both about the preludes themselves and about this very process of rediscovery. Such rediscovery involves the stimulation and exercise of what may be new musical "muscles" for some: asking provocative questions, reading "between the lines," and attempting to enter the mind of Chopin as he decides to go here instead of there, this way instead of that. These pursuits involve imaginative and creative skills that we often neglect in the face of the enormous challenges of refined pianism, but I believe we neglect them at great cost to our musical souls.

Thus, the user of this edition may expect to encounter many questions throughout the performance notes, some answered, some left unanswered. The goal of such questions is not just to provide information but also to stimulate creative thinking. There is indeed much to think about, and learning how to think well about music is an essential aspect of learning to play it well. Asking skillful questions – reading "between the lines" – getting inside the mind of the composer: these are the overarching motives of this new edition.

The Score and the Recording

I have based this edition on the manuscript Chopin completed in Majorca in January of 1839, and although the manuscript is not entirely free of errors, as we shall see, it is unusually beautiful and instructive. I present the information contained in this manuscript in all its elegant economy. Dynamics, slurs, pedal indications, verbal directions, hairpin *crescendos* and *diminuendos*, even Chopin's sometimes surprising chord and note spellings, all have been meticulously reproduced. I have changed, or added, very little. The very few changes are without exception noted and explained in the performance notes. The occasional additions are solely for the purpose of clarifying Chopin's intentions where the manuscript leaves them incomplete or in doubt, and are usually set in brackets. Where brackets are not feasible, the additions are explained in the notes.

I wish to acknowledge, in addition to the manuscript, the reference sources I've consulted to create this edition: the (Polish) National Edition of Jan Ekier, and the Henle Urtext. I have also learned an enormous amount from the extensive commentary in the Paderewski edition and have benefited from an examination of the edition of Chopin's pupil Carl Mikuli.

Another source that has guided my work on this edition is the knowledge gained from the "field of play," the concert stage. I have performed these works for many years and have also recorded them, and I am eager to pass on what this experience has taught me.

I would like to comment here on the recording included in this edition. For an aspiring artist, listening to any CD recording represents something of a danger and an opportunity. The opportunity is that a sound picture, no less than a visual one, is worth the proverbial thousand words. The danger is that the listener might take the recording too literally and attempt to copy exactly what I have done, undermining my primary aim of guiding the pianist to his or her own personal and creative relationship with the *Preludes*. Listeners should bear in mind that the recording offers one possible realization among many, a musical snapshot if you will, taken in January of 2001. A performer's career encompasses an entire "album" of such snapshots, and no two of these will be identical, for performers are themselves students who continue to learn and discover throughout their lives, always adding new layers of understanding. My work on this edition has added many such layers.

Fingering

When I considered the issue of fingerings for this edition, I settled on the motto: "First show them how I might solve the problem, then let them solve it for themselves." As a teacher, I am acutely aware of the danger of offering too much assistance when a student is eager to solve his or her own problems. Hence, I offer most fingering suggestions toward the beginning of a prelude and pass the baton to the user of this edition toward the end. Of course, there is always more than one way to finger a passage well. What I offer are suggestions only, and frequently a second possibility is noted in parentheses.

Pianists may note my fondness for finger substitutions. There are several accounts of Chopin's having instructed his own students to strive for a sensuous relationship between the fingers and the keys. For example, as Jean-Jacques Eigeldinger reports in *Chopin: Pianist and Teacher* (1986), Chopin advised one student to "caress the key, never bash it." Finger substitutions are one way of cultivating this caress, often involving a delicious slide along the key.

Pedaling

Pedaling was without doubt the most problematic issue throughout the preparation of this edition. The problems derived from the inherent inexactness of the symbols Chopin used, a slightly flowery "ped." for depression (𝄢.) and a large oval with a cross through it for release (⊕), to say nothing of his occasional mild sloppiness. For example, sometimes the music for each hand is placed at slightly different points along a horizontal axis, and one is left wondering whether a pedal mark is meant to occur at the appropriate point in the left or right hand. Chopin famously disliked the tedium of writing down his ideas. By the time he was ready to add pedal markings he may well have been too tired of the whole process to care much about precision.

Rather than leave the markings in this state of imprecision, I have chosen to use a clear, modern pedal indication, a horizontal line with precise depress and release points. ⌐_____∧_____∧_____⌐ This also makes continuous *legato* pedaling easy to represent.

When interpreting Chopin's pedal markings, the pianist must keep in mind a historical factor concerning the type of piano Chopin used in comparison to today's instruments. Although advances in piano construction considerably increased the expressive potential of pianos in Chopin's time, modern cast-iron frames were not integral to their structure until the mid-19th century. With the heavier metal frame came a great deal more tension on the strings, much more power in the projection of tone, and greater blur in longer pedaling. Chopin, writing for instruments with weaker frames, often wrote longer pedal markings than would normally be employed on today's instruments.

In spite of these historical factors, I have chosen to translate Chopin's pedal markings as faithfully and accurately as possible into our precise indications. The pianist deserves, after all, to be aware of Chopin's original intentions. Where these markings would seem less appropriate for modern instruments, or where Chopin's indications seem incomplete, I offer alternative suggestions under the heading "Pedaling Possibilities" in the individual performance notes.

Ornamentation

I suggest a non-dogmatic approach regarding the interpretation of ornaments in Chopin's Preludes. The very nature of ornamentation places it in the realm of the spontaneous, the improvised, where Chopin of course reigned supreme. It is unlikely that he ever played ornaments exactly the same way twice. That said, I have reproduced Chopin's ornamentation exactly as he wrote it in the manuscript, even when he writes similar ornaments in different ways within the same prelude.

I also follow precisely Chopin's inclusion or exclusion of cross-strokes on all grace notes. However, one may fairly ask what significance these cross-strokes have in Chopin's music, since he was far from consistent in their use. The answer is likely, "only a little." Broadly speaking, there are four possibilities for the execution of grace notes, whether they have cross-strokes or not. They may be played quickly before the beat, quickly on the beat, slowly (or at least more expressively) before the beat, and slowly (or more expressively) on the beat. The presence or absence of a cross-stroke may provide a clue to the intended execution of a grace note. It does seem to me that Chopin is somewhat more likely to use cross-strokes in faster tempos, where the ornaments are likely to be played quickly and before the beat. Where he does not use cross-strokes, the grace notes seem somewhat more likely intended as appoggiaturas, to be played expressively, and on the beat. However, there are exceptions; hence the non-dogmatic approach.

Several ornaments in Preludes warrant further discussion. Shorter ones have been realized in the score itself. Prelude No. 9 merits special consideration due to variant rhythmic notations for its signature rhythmic figure.

Example A (first edition):

The first edition and many subsequent publications notate this rhythmic figure as shown above, with the sixteenth note set apart from the lower-voice triplet throughout. This notation implies that the sixteenth note is to be played after the final eighth of the triplet, and indeed, it is most often performed that way. However, in Chopin's manuscript this figure is written as in Example B below, allowing for a different interpretation.

Example B (manuscript):

Note that in this version, the sixteenth note is to be played simultaneously with the final eighth of the triplet. If the performer adopts this version of the prelude, I recommend that the upper voice in beat 1, m. 8, be played as a duplet against the lower-voice triplet:

***Prelude No. 9:* m. 8, beats 1-2**

For m. 4, the usual execution, following the first-edition version, is as follows, with the grace notes before the trill played either on the beat or before the beat:

***Prelude No. 9:* m. 4, beat 4**

However, if the manuscript variant is applied, the ornament may be played thus:

***Prelude No. 9:* m. 4, beat 4**

If the first-edition notation is followed, the ornamental notes that follow the trill should be played with the sixteenth note.

***Prelude No. 9:* m. 3, beats 3-4; m. 4, beat 1**

But if the manuscript's rhythmic interpretation is adopted:

Prelude No. 9: m. 3, beats 3-4; m. 4, beat 1

The final LH notes of m. 3 may also be played after the final RH chord.

In sum, many factors should be considered when deciding how to execute a Chopin ornament: the mood of the prelude, the level of dissonance in the ornament, the tempo, the presence or absence of cross-strokes, historical performance practice, etc. The student or performer should experiment with various possibilities and then have a good reason for his or her choice. I will make frequent recommendations in the individual performance notes.

Phrase Structure

In the individual notes for each prelude, I suggest a possible diagram of the phrase structure for consideration. It is particularly interesting to note where Chopin departs from the usual 4- or 8-bar phrase. When a longer phrase encompasses several smaller segments, I place a possible segmentation in parentheses. Particularly interesting phrase or segment lengths are noted with an exclamation point. The structure is outlined quite broadly, however, in groups of whole measures. The student is encouraged to parse the phrase structure in greater detail.

The Individual Preludes

PRELUDE NO. 2

Chopin gives no harmonic clue as to the key of this prelude until the 15th measure, and the only A minor chord is the final one. This may have been one of the preludes to inspire the well-known Schumann review of Op. 28, in which he calls the *Preludes* "remarkable [*merkwürdig*, which can also connote 'strange']" and compares them to "ruins, individual eagle pinions, all disorder and wild confusion." (I quote Jeffrey Kallberg's excellent article on the *Preludes* in *The Cambridge Companion to Chopin* (1992), edited by Chopin scholar Jim Samson.)

One wonders: Did Chopin set out to compose a piece with the tonic chord delayed to the latest possible moment, or did the piece naturally unfold that way in the spirit of improvisation? Was it Chopin's intent to leave the listener disturbed by such tonal ambiguity, as Schumann probably was? This question can lead us to an inquiry into the very nature of composing. How much is consciously decided ahead of time? Is disturbance a legitimate purpose of art? Does the tonal ambiguity in this piece disturb you?

Note that Chopin's opening notation suggests that he intends the B-A♯-B-G (etc.) "middle voice" of the left-hand accompaniment to possess its own melodic integrity, perhaps as a brooding counterpoint to the main theme soon to emerge. I believe he returns to a simpler notation for convenience, and not because the voice in question loses its melodic character. Bear this initial notation in mind throughout the prelude. For example, here is how m. 6 would look if notated similarly.

Prelude No. 2: m. 6, l.h.

Observe how the notation highlights the melodic character of the "inner voice."

M. 5: I recommend a slow and expressive appoggiatura here and elsewhere in this prelude, played on the beat (meaning in this case simultaneous with the fourth eighth) and about equal to a triplet sixteenth.

M. 18: *Slentando* is similar in Italian to *rallentando*. Note the shared root of the words, *lento*, or slow.

M. 21: Chopin's use of the word *sostenuto* here may suggest a slightly more measured, tenderly deliberate tempo. The word means "sustained" in Italian.

MM. 22, 23: I believe the arpeggiated chords in these measures are most expressive if rolled on the beat. I also recommend holding the upbeat to m. 23 (the middle C), until the last note of the final chord is played, thus maintaining a melodic *legato*.

Pedaling Possibilities
The pedal may be used, broadly speaking, for three general purposes at the piano: the combination of tones, connection between tones (i.e. legato), and coloring of tones. I refer to these

as "the three Cs of pedaling." Although Chopin gives only one pedal marking in this prelude, in mm. 18-19, this does not necessarily mean we are not to pedal elsewhere. Rather, I interpret this single pedal mark as Chopin's only explicit request to combine tones in the prelude. The pianist may use the pedal for deeper legato and richer tone color for much of this prelude, and perhaps throughout. Acknowledge Chopin's pedaling here by combining tones quite sparingly (if at all), apart from mm. 18-19.

Possible Phrase Structure
1-7 (1-2, 3-7!); 8-12!; 13-23! (13-19! 20-23)

For Further Exploration
One of the more useful questions we can ask of a musical moment is: "What is occurring here for the first time?" When in doubt about what is interesting or beautiful at any moment in a work, try asking that question. Ask that of m. 17 in this prelude. Then ask the same of m. 19, then m. 20. With a little practice, we can find something new about virtually every measure. Every such "event," or novelty, contributes to the story the music tells, and the more conscious we are of these musical events, the more vivid and alive the story.

There are two instances of syncopation in the melodic line in this prelude. Can you find them both? Are they alike or different from each other?

PRELUDE NO. 4
Chopin demonstrates his unique contrapuntal gift in this prelude. This in unquestionably a prelude of great melodic beauty, and yet if we play the right hand by itself the line feels static, almost dull. Chopin give the line life by creating great interest in the LH chords, and in so doing invests the accompaniment with a counter-melodic strength. With each successive chord change, one (or occasionally two) of the chordal notes descends a whole, or more commonly, a half step. The descent occurs in no particular pattern and in no discernible order, resulting in many chords that do not function according to traditional harmonic practice, and herein lies their fascination. For example, in a work in E minor, we would expect the left-hand D7 chord in m. 7 to resolve to the relative-major key of G if it were functioning normally. In this prelude's tonal world, this chord functions entirely differently, but with no less convincing a musical logic. The static right-hand melodic line "borrows," as it were, the compelling allure of the throbbing left-hand chords. The melodic line comes into its own

more vivid beauty around m. 8, precisely when the chords below return to traditional tonal function, no longer needed for their nonfunctional fascination. This is an entirely different counterpoint from that of Chopin's first love, Bach, the contrapuntal master *nonpareil*, and yet it is clearly informed and inspired by it.

The word *largo* means "broad" in Italian. The three preludes marked *largo* (the E major, C minor, and this one) suggest that for Chopin (at least in the *Preludes*) *largo* indicates a striding tempo with a broad "gait." (In general, Chopin's *lento* would seem to indicate a somewhat slower tempo. See the note for Prelude No. 6.) Keep in mind that this prelude is to be felt broadly in two, not in four, as it is marked C or "cut time."

Compare the accompaniment of this prelude to that of the *Mazurka in A minor, Op. 17, No. 4*, composed a few years before the *Preludes*. That mazurka may have been a kind of creative seed for this prelude.

Mazurka, Op. 17, No. 4: mm. 8-11, l.h.

Prelude No. 4: mm. 1-4, l.h.

Identifying similar passages or principles in different works is one of the keys to entering the mental processes of the composer.

MM. 8, 12: No better illustrations exist for my adage, "A Chopin accent is always more than an accent," than the two accents in these measures. Can you find something novel about these accented notes, something which may have inspired Chopin to accent them, beyond the call, simply, for greater volume? This novelty is the key to interpreting the accent convincingly. Consider m. 12: Notice that the accented C is the first note since the chords were introduced in m. 1 to be played *without accompaniment*. Awareness of this might encourage the performer to play this lonely note more soulfully and more searchingly, perhaps even more painfully, than the surrounding notes, and not merely more loudly.

Can you see what is novel about the G♯ of m. 8? (See the Appendix for a possible answer.)

Alternatively, it is possible to interpret the accents in these measures as *diminuendo* "hairpins," rather than accents. Often the two are indistinguishable in Chopin's manuscripts, and one must use context and instinct to determine his intent. Different interpretations are valid. For example, both the Henle edition and that of Chopin's pupil Carl Mikuli interpret the mark in m. 8 as a *diminuendo*, and both editions consider the mark in m. 12 an accent. Ekier gives the marks in *both* measures as accents, as does Paderewski, but in Ekier's edition they are slightly larger than normal size.

M. 12: What makes this measure so poignantly beautiful? I believe it has something to do with the close juxtaposition of the raised 7th degree of the scale and the lowered 7th, in this case the D♯ and the D♮. This is a favorite expressive device of Chopin's.

Prelude No. 4: m. 12, r.h.

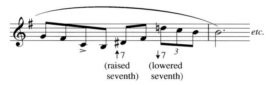

Can you find other instances of this juxtaposition in the *Preludes*?

M. 14: Consider that there are often slight differences between otherwise similar phrases. For example, compare m. 14 to m. 2 and note the expressive difference. Sometimes, listening deeply and responding *consciously* to the difference between varied points in similar phrases is all that is necessary to project that difference beautifully and convincingly. To focus on these subtle differences, juxtapose them, playing them immediately after one another. For example, here play m. 2, and then immediately play m. 14. As you play, be conscious of the difference between the two phrases, and your listener will be as well.

M. 24: This is the first instance of the dynamic *pianissimo* in the *Preludes*. Be sure to highlight it.

Pedaling Possibilities
It seems odd that Chopin indicates only two instances of pedal in this prelude. The two instances share something in common: They involve the only departures from repeated chords in the accompaniment. In both cases, the LH descends for a deeper bass-anchor that Chopin wants sustained. However, I believe this prelude

offers evidence that Chopin sometimes considers use of the pedal to be so obvious that its explicit indication is unnecessary. Note the slurs over the LH chords, suggesting a *legato* articulation. This *legato* would be impossible with repeated chords if no pedal were used at all. Experiment with light *legato* pedal, changing it fractionally on every eighth note, or changing less frequently (for a richer sound) to taste. The final chords can use a deeper pedal for *legato* and resonance.

Possible Phrase Structure
MM. 1-12 (1-4, 5-8, 9-12); 13-25 (13-16, 17-20, 21-25)

For Further Exploration
What is extraordinary about the first chord in this prelude?

Have you ever spelled a word wrong on a test? Is there a chord in this prelude which Chopin may have "misspelled"? What does it mean to misspell a chord?

PRELUDE NO. 6
"There is one [prelude] that came to him through an evening of dismal rain—it casts the soul into a terrible dejection." (I quote Thomas Higgins' translation of George Sand's *Histoire de Ma Vie*, a passage of which appears in the *Norton Critical Score* of the *Preludes*, Higgins, ed.) It is hard to imagine that these words of George Sand refer to the soothing prelude we have come to know as the "Raindrop," No. 15. Although she does not specify to which prelude she refers, many now believe she was writing of this one, No. 6. The expressive repeated-note motive in this prelude may recall a steady, mournful rainfall, though it is doubtful that Chopin himself was inspired by the sound of rain. The title "Raindrop" is certainly not Chopin's, for this or any prelude. He was not fond of fanciful titles, and protested when Sand attempted to connect a musical event in his works with an explicit extra-musical inspiration. However, a concrete mental image or metaphor is frequently helpful to the student and performer, as it can inspire interpretive creativity and bring to life a more vivid tonal imagery. For example, in this prelude, the accents can be interpreted to suggest a throbbing quality in the repeated notes.

Often, pianists must determine whether a composer leaves out markings because he truly wishes them absent or because he believes the performer will understand them to be assumed. This prelude offers an intriguing example of such a conundrum, and again the manuscript is instructive. The accents and slurs of m. 1 would seem to apply to all beats of similar right-hand motivic structure throughout the prelude, perhaps ending with m. 22. However, the manuscript tells a different and rather puzzling story. Chopin at first placed accents and slurs in what seems to be an all but haphazard manner throughout the prelude, in apparent defiance of any intuitive musical logic. To cite one example, he added accents and slurs identical to those in m. 1 through the second beat of m. 6, but omitted them from mm. 9 and 10 when the theme returns, only to include them in several subsequent measures. Moreover, sometimes he included the slur but no accent, again with no apparent musical logic. Then he went to the trouble of crossing out all such markings except those in m. 1 and on the third beat of m. 22. I believe the first lesson to be drawn from this is simply: when markings are absent, be very careful what you assume! Second, I suggest that Chopin made a deliberate choice not to "micromanage" the performer's musicianship, but rather to respect his or her interpretive prerogative. He leaves the accented, slurred pulsing of repeated notes, or their non-pulsing (beyond those marked), to the instincts of the performer.

M. 7: In the general prefatory comments, I suggest a non-dogmatic approach to the interpretation of grace notes in Chopin's *Preludes*. The two in this measure provide an excellent opportunity for such freedom of interpretation. These grace notes are the first of the *Preludes* to have cross-strokes. Although cross-strokes on grace notes as used by Chopin frequently imply a faster execution, I play the first of the two expressively and before the beat. I prefer to play the second one faster, and also before the beat. Experiment with several possibilities before settling on your preference.

M. 19: It is impossible to say whether the middle note of the right-hand chord on beat 2 of this measure is an F♯ or a G in Chopin's manuscript. Ekier interprets the note as an F♯; in Henle, Paderewski and other editions the note is a G.

M. 26: It is interesting to note that this, the slowest of all the *Preludes*, is the first to end without a *fermata*. Perhaps Chopin felt that with the slower tempo, no extra time is called for in the final silence of the prelude.

Pedaling Possibilities
Again Chopin seems to have written explicit pedal markings only when they involve a relatively significant combination of tones, leaving them out as unnecessary when the pedal is to be used for legato or for coloring. I recommend pedaling through the full beat when four arpeggiated 16ths are played; otherwise, I recommend legato pedaling once, twice, or up to four times per beat as called for by the melodic line and the taste of the performer.

Possible Phrase Structure
1-8 (1-2, 3-4, 5-8); 9-14! (9-10, 11-12, 13-14), 15-18, 19-22, 23-26

For Further Exploration
Like many great composers, Chopin was a lover of the lowered supertonic (i.e. flattened II) or Neapolitan triad. Found most often in first inversion, it is usually symbolized "N6" for that reason, and it usually leads to the dominant, often passing first through the tonic 6/4 chord. The darker color of the lowered supertonic offers a particularly expressive path to the dominant. Can you find an extended phrase in the key of the Neapolitan in this prelude? Is the triad itself used in first inversion? Does the phrase lead to the dominant? There are many instances of the Neapolitan in the Preludes. This is the first.

In Prelude No. 4 we saw the raised seventh (i.e. the leading-tone) followed closely and expressively by the lowered seventh. Can you find a similar expressive device in this prelude? How does this instance differ from the earlier example?

PRELUDE NO. 7
This is a miniature mazurka! One of the characteristic mazurka rhythms is a dotted-eighth/sixteenth note on the first beat of a 3/4 measure, and we see that rhythm consistently here.

Prelude No. 7: mm. 1-2, r.h.

Mazurka, Op. 17, No. 4: mm. 5-6, r.h.

The second example above is excerpted from the opening measures of the *Mazurka in A Minor, Op. 17, No. 4*, also cited in the notes for Prelude No. 4. Note the rhythmic similarity of the two examples.

For Chopin, the marking *Andantino* suggested a tempo slightly faster than *Andante*. However, it is worth noting that in the manuscript Chopin appears to have written *Andante* originally. He then crossed it out and wrote *Andantino* instead. It may be valid, therefore, to perform this prelude on the slower side of *Andantino*, in recognition of Chopin's original impulse.

Given that this is one of the shortest works that Chopin ever composed, it is worth considering here the nature of Chopin's genius for brevity. One essential characteristic of this genius is the knowledge of *what to leave out*. For an imagination as fertile as Chopin's, this is no small matter. There is an amusing illustration of this phenomenon in the literary world. The French mathematician and philosopher Blaise Pascal once wrote an exceptionally long letter to a friend, at the end of which he apologized because *he didn't have time to write a shorter one!*

Pedaling Possibilities

The construction of the modern piano is relevant to the performance of this prelude. On a modern instrument, the pedaling as Chopin gives it usually sounds to blurred. I recommend a slight clearance of the pedal just after the dotted rhythm, lifting up the pedal about one-half of the way before re-depressing it.

Prelude No. 7: mm. 1-4

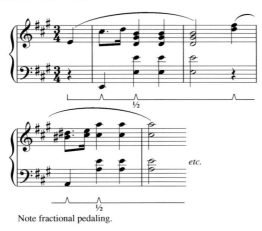

Note fractional pedaling.

Also, as this excerpt shows, I recommend pedaling from the pickup to the downbeat (where Chopin indicates no pedal), both for consistency of sound and also for a better legato when the pickup and the downbeat are the same notes. Change the pedal, of course, on the downbeat.

Possible Phrase Structure

MM. 1-8 (1-4, 5-8); 9-16 (9-12, 13-16)

For Further Exploration

This prelude offers an opportunity to develop an important aspect of musical insight: the capacity to see something new in comparable phrases. The performer who remains conscious of these nuances throughout the piece will communicate them to the listener, who will be aware of them as elements of an unfolding story. In each of the eight phrase segments, determine what is happening for the first time. (See also the note for Prelude No. 2.)

PRELUDE NO. 9

The rhythm of this prelude has long posed a conundrum to editors and performers. A full debate of all elements of this conundrum is best left to another forum. Here I will outline the decision the performer must make and offer a rationale for either of the two possible choices.

In his manuscript, Chopin consistently notates the right-hand sixteenth notes directly above the third chord of the eighth-note triplets, joining the sixteenth and the lower notes into a chord with a single stem. It is hard to avoid the conclusion that Chopin intends these sixteenths to be played simultaneously with the lower notes, in Baroque style. In no case, to my knowledge, does Chopin notate with a single stem notes he intended to be played sequentially. But the earliest editions of the Preludes, published during Chopin's lifetime, consistently notate the sixteenth offset from the triplet.

Prelude No. 9: m. 1, beat 2, r.h.

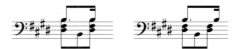

The edition of Carl Mikuli, still in widespread use to this day, is of particular interest, as Mikuli had been a student of Chopin. His edition offsets the 16ths, as do most subsequent editions. Why this discrepancy?

One clue may be found in the manuscript itself. There is one single beat that has always raised strong doubts about the Baroque interpretation, beat one of m. 8. Despite the fact that the notes in the upper voice in this beat are not the usual dotted rhythm but two equal eighths, Chopin notates the beat exactly like the dotted rhythms in terms of stemming and vertical alignment. Here would seem to be evidence that, in this prelude at least, alignment and stemming alone do not dictate execution, since surely Chopin did not intend the dotted cases and the undotted case to be played identically. This beat, I suggest, may have constituted at least in part the justification for offsetting the sixteenth notes in the engraving of the first and subsequent editions.

A case can thus be made both for offsetting the sixteenth in performance, and for playing the sixteenth simultaneously with the third eighth. Consequently, while we print the traditional interpretation offsetting the sixteenths, we offer both possibilities to the performer and encourage his or her choice between the two. However, I urge the performer to take into account the necessity of distinguishing between the dotted rhythms and the single undotted rhythm of m. 8, beat one. How may this be done? If the performer chooses the traditional interpretation, offsetting the sixteenths, it is easy to distinguish this beat: one simply plays it exactly as it is notated in the manuscript, with the second eighth of the upper voice played simultaneously with the third eighth of the triplet. However, if the Baroque interpretation is chosen, in which all sixteenths are played simultaneously with the third eighth of the triplet, it is more difficult to see how one may distinguish m. 8, beat one. Here the Mikuli edition provides a solution: in this beat, the upper voice eighth notes are engraved as a duplet independent of the lower-voice triplet, positioned so as to represent a clear two-against-three rhythm.

The entire issue may therefore be summarized as follows: If the performer follows the traditional approach, offset the sixteenths when the rhythm is dotted and make the second eighth in the upper voice of the first beat of m. 8 coincide with the third eighth of the lower-voice triplet. If the Baroque interpretation implied by Chopin's manuscript is followed, play the sixteenth simultaneously with the third eighth of the triplet when the rhythm is dotted, and play the upper voice as a duplet against the lower-voice triplet in the first beat of m. 8.

If the performer follows the traditional approach, I caution that the sixteenth not be made equal to half of a triplet eighth, but rather represent a true sixteenth (i.e. one fourth of a quarter) against the triplet accompaniment. I recommend that the 32nd notes equal one half of a true sixteenth (i.e. one eighth of a quarter note). It is worth noting that the Ekier edition, which adopts the manuscript's version (i.e. the Baroque interpretation), recommends that the 32nd notes be made to equal to one half of the triplet eighth, or one sixth of a quarter note.

Consult the section marked "Ornamentation" above for examples illustrating the above points.

Chopin uses the evolving rhythms in the melodic line, from single- to double-dotted, to underscore the increasing stateliness in this most majestic of the *Preludes*. I believe this unusually important rhythmic role was carefully intended by Chopin to follow Prelude No. 8, in which rhythmic evolution plays no role whatsoever.

M. 8: Chopin adds the word "*decresc.*" to the hairpin *diminuendo* in this measure. The word begins at the C-flat, and dashes extend it to the end of the measure. Because the word appears redundant with the hairpin, I decided to remove it from the score for purposes of visual clarity. However, it is possible that Chopin intended the use of both the word and the hairpin as a form of emphasis. Make the *decrescendo* a vivid one!

M. 11: Again Chopin includes both the hairpin and the word "cresc." in this measure. Because the hairpin, which begins directly on the downbeat, lasts only for two beats here, while the cresc. is extended by dashes to last the whole measure, I removed the hairpin in this case for added visual clarity. It is possible, again, that Chopin includes both the word and the hairpin for emphasis, and again I recommend that the *crescendo* be unusually vivid.

M. 12: To the half-note E in the bass on the downbeat of this measure, I add a quarter-note E on the same pitch and the same beat, following Paderewski's example. The quarter note accounts visually for the voice that moves to B on the second beat.

Pedaling Possibilities
Chopin sometimes indicates pedaling through harmonic changes in this prelude. On modern instruments I recommend at least half-changes of the pedal (if not more) when the harmony changes. It is also possible to pedal lightly for added majesty, *legato* and sound consistency where Chopin indicates no pedaling. Pay close attention however, to the quality of your finger *legato* where Chopin does not notate pedal.

Possible Phrase Structure
1-4 (1-2, 3-4); 5-8; 9-12!

For Further Exploration
Chopin was a master of harmonic innovation and experimentation. There are two very interesting harmonic approaches to the dominant in this prelude. Can you find them both?

How might you attempt to tell the rhythmic story of this prelude in words? It might start out with a rhythmic disagreement between the hands. Where would it go from there?

PRELUDE NO. 15

One may presume that Chopin's undeserved reputation among some listeners as an effete composer is due at least in part to the frequent excerpting of this very beautiful prelude. Taken alone, it is one of Chopin's more tender and heartfelt utterances, quite accessible to the untrained ear, and within reach, technically, of the early intermediate piano student. However, if heard too often, it can seem ingratiatingly sweet. It is my firm conviction, however, that to fully appreciate this work one must taste its sweetness in context, both preceded by the demonic Prelude No. 14 and followed by the colossus of the *Preludes*, No. 16. Imagine attributing those preludes to an effete composer! Again I cite this need for context as evidence that Chopin conceived of the *Preludes* as a whole, greater than the sum of its parts, in which no individual prelude can be appreciated optimally without its neighbors.

The instruction *sostenuto* appears at a tender moment within the body of Prelude No. 13, accompanied by the words *più lento*. Here, I believe we may take the unusual tempo marking to imply the creation of a sound world of deep sentiment and affection, marked by a subtle reluctance to move ahead and leave each lovely phrase behind. Although Chopin occasionally used the word sostenuto to modify tempo markings (most often in the *Nocturnes*), I have found only one other of his works that bears the sole word *Sostenuto* as its tempo marking, the *Prelude in C-sharp minor*, Op. 45.

I recommend playing the grace notes before the beat in mm. 4, 11 (and similar measures), and 39.

M. 2: I have followed closely the notation of Chopin's manuscript of this prelude. Note Chopin's consistent notation in this and similar measures: the C is a dotted half note; the E♭ and G♭ are half notes. However, I do not believe it is necessary to make excessive efforts to release the E♭ and G♭ precisely at the third beat. Rather, I believe Chopin is implying a "finger pedal" for added sonorous richness. In any case, Chopin's pedal markings clearly extend the E♭ and G♭ beyond the notated values. (Note that use of finger pedal may be concurrent with use of the foot pedal.) On the other hand, I do urge the

performer to adhere strictly to the holding of voices as notated, as with the leading tone (i.e., middle C) in mm. 3 and 4. Such examples of tonal fullness through the use of finger pedal help to offset the monotony threatened by the repetition of the A♭, or fifth degree of the tonic chord. Carefully note all examples of finger pedal in this prelude, e.g. the extra-stemmed A♭ in mm. 3, 7 and elsewhere, and the extra-stemmed G♭ of m. 19.

MM. 4, 23 and 79: I recommend that the grouplets in these measures be allowed to unfold spontaneously in the spirit of an improvised decoration. Alternatively, they may be measured or apportioned more strictly, according to individual preference. The examples below illustrate two possible realizations, the first more freely performed, and the second, more strictly measured:

Prelude No. 15: m. 4, beats 3-4

Prelude No. 15: m. 23, beats 3-4

Prelude No. 15: m. 79, beats 3-4

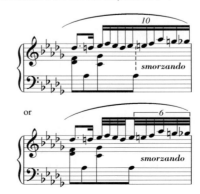

M. 17: It is doubtful whether there is truly an E♭ just below the higher F on the last beat of this measure in Chopin's manuscript, (though it is possible to read it thus). We have, however, followed Henle's example in including this note analogously with mm. 11 and 15. Ekier leaves the note out.

MM. 28-30, 44-46: In his manuscript, Chopin used a hairpin to indicate the *crescendo* through these measures, adding the apparently redundant word "*cresc.*," with dashes, in m. 30. It is possible that Chopin intended the hairpin and the word "*cresc.*" to join emphatically in m. 30. However, I have removed the apparent redundancy for visual clarity, choosing to represent the entire crescendo over the three bars solely with the word "*cresc.*" and dashes. See the note for Prelude No. 9.

MM. 33, 49: The final beat in the left hand is an octave C♯ in the manuscript. I have retained that here, though Paderewski reports in his edition that Chopin changed the lower C♯ to the E a third above it in a copy of the first French edition. (The E is the note you will hear in my recording.) Though it occurs twice in the piece, the manuscript affords only one chance to view the measure, as Chopin did not re-notate mm. 44-58.

M. 63: Note the opportunity for expressiveness as the repeated G♯ finally becomes dissonant and is resolved, first to F♯, and then to A, the first and third degrees of the subdominant triad, respectively.

M. 68: It is a mystery to me why Chopin briefly adds a left-hand repetition of the G♯ in this measure to join that of the right hand, and yet it is one of my favorite moments in this prelude. Because we cannot know the "why" of this lovely unexpected twist (and indeed a "why" may not exist), it has become for me a sort of enigmatic greeting mid-performance from the composer, a kind of musical "wink."

MM. 79, 80, 88: It is worth noting that the "*-ndo*" and "*-to*" endings in Italian are the gerund (acting as a present participle) and past participle, respectively. Therefore, words like *crescendo* and *diminuendo* refer to a change in process, and words such as *animato* and *ritenuto* refer to a change already attained. *Smorzando* may be translated literally as "lessening," or more poetically "dying away," and is clearly a process. *Ritenuto* differs from *slentando* in that the former is an attained state —"held back"— and the latter is in process — "getting slower." Although literal

interpretations are not always necessary (and composers themselves do not always know the precise meanings of the Italian words they use), it is, I believe, important to understand the literal meanings of such directives, and then interpret them responsibly and thoughtfully through the prism of one's convictions, bearing in mind the context in which the words are used.

M. 87: As Chopin set the E♭ significantly apart from the C and G♭ in the right hand, there is no doubt as to which note receives the accent: the E♭. Note that it is not rare for Chopin to disdain, in his manuscripts, the vertical alignment of simultaneous musical events.

Pedaling Possibilities
I do not, as I have stated before, believe it is necessary to avoid the use of the pedal where Chopin does not indicate it. I believe, however, that we must orient our use of the pedal in such instances toward the enhancement of *legato* and the coloring of tone, rather than toward the combination of tones. In other words, the pedal is used primarily for only two of the three "C's" of pedaling. (See the note for Prelude No. 2.) Thus the use of the pedal where it is not noted is generally lighter and more discreet than where noted. In particular, pay close attention to the quality of your finger *legato* in the passage from mm. 28-39, and in the similar passage later.

Chopin did not indicate a pedal release at the *forte* in m. 81. As there is no release indication anywhere before the next ***p*** it was clearly an oversight on Chopin's part. The question is where Chopin intended the release. Several possibilities exist: experiment with extending the pedal into the forte with infrequent changes; for example, hold the pedal through m. 82, then change the pedal on the downbeat of m. 83. Another possibility, which I favor, is a deep *legato* pedal, one change per quarter note, from the *forte* through m. 83.

Possible Phrase Structure
1-8 (1-4, 5-8); 9-19! (9-12, 13-16, 17-19!); 20-27 (20-23, 24-27); 28-35; 36-43 (36-39, 40-43); 44-51; 52-59 (52-55, 56-59); 60-67 (60-63, 64-67); 68-75 (68-73! 74-75); 76-89! (76-79, 80-83, 84-89)

For Further Exploration
Chopin seems to have set himself a compositional challenge, in the form of a limit, in this prelude. What is that challenge? Put another way, he adopted the musical equivalent of a poet's rhyme scheme. What is that scheme?

PRELUDE NO. 20

Although Chopin apparently preferred composing dances to marches, two of his best known, best loved works are marches: the "Funeral March" of the second sonata, and this prelude, also funereal. One of Chopin's large-scale masterpieces is a march, but it is not so entitled: the *Fantasy, Op. 49*. It too begins funereally, but eventually reaches luminous heights. Almost all of the handful of *Marches* written by Chopin are funeral in whole or part. Can you think of other works of Chopin that are march-like (or have march-like passages)? Prelude No. 9 is rare for Chopin in being a joyous march throughout.

It is quite unusual for Chopin to begin a work *fortissimo*. Not a single etude, for example, begins *fortissimo*, and this is the only prelude to begin thus. Chopin was a consummate storyteller, and to begin a work *fortissimo* is, in effect, to begin at a high point of the story. This rarely works in literature or in music. I see this as another piece of evidence that Chopin conceived of the 24 Preludes as an organic whole, for Prelude No. 20 would seem to need its predecessors as preparation for its aural power. Furthermore, the last two chords of Prelude No. 19 represent, to my ears, a kind of "seed" of what is to follow in Prelude No. 20.

The performer must make a clear distinction between *forte* and *fortissimo* throughout the *Preludes*. Be sure to relate the initial sound level in this prelude to *fortes* and *fortissimos* found in other preludes. Make no apologies for Chopin's rare *fortissimo* opening here. Likewise, be sure to distinguish clearly between the *piano* and *pianissimo* of the repeated second phrase. Ernest Hutcheson points out, in his book *The Literature of the Piano* (1966), that this distinction between *piano* and *pianissimo* is just as important as that between *forte* and *piano*.

M. 3: It is impossible to know with certainty whether the final chord of this measure was intended by Chopin to be minor or major. Apparently he inserted the flat before the last E of the measure in a student's copy of the *Preludes*. It is possible to find fine editions and recordings that give it in major and equally fine editions and recordings that give it in minor. Therefore, I recommend that performers decide for themselves which reading they prefer. They may even play it differently on different occasions, perhaps not even knowing themselves which

chord they'll choose until the moment arrives. I have done this myself, though I prefer the minor and usually play it as such.

MM. 7-12: Chopin notated mm. 5-8 only once in the manuscript, indicating in his usual manner the repetition of the phrase for mm. 9-12. However, he made clear that the *ritenuto* is intended for both statements of the phrase, and the crescendo only for the second. His manner of indicating this repetition almost certainly accounts for his having forgotten to include an "*a tempo*" after the first *ritenuto*. I have placed the *a tempo* in m. 9 in brackets.

M. 12: Observe the root-position Neapolitan chord in the penultimate measure. Chopin is unabashed here about the resulting unusual, stark tritone in the bass octaves on beats 2 and 3.

Pedaling Possibilities

Chopin indicated no pedaling whatsoever in this prelude until the final cadence. There can be no more convincing evidence of the likelihood that Chopin sometimes considers the use of the pedal to be assumed for legato and coloring where no pedal is explicitly marked. I recommend legato pedaling once per beat. Highly skilled pianists may experiment with pedal changes for all melodic notes, including the sixteenths. In this case, make sure the fingers hold all quarter notes through the pedal changes on the sixteenths.

Possible Phrase Structure

1-4 (1! 2! 3-4); 5-8 (5! 6! 7! 8!); 9-12 (simile); 13!

For Further Exploration

As Thomas Higgins points out in his "Notes Toward a Performance" of the *Preludes*, Chopin rather humorously added a note in the manuscript implying that it was on the advice of a certain "Monsieur xxx who is often right" that he repeated the second phrase. How does this repetition leave the piece with an unusual structure?

PRELUDE NO. 22

Teachers often ask their students which hand or voice is the most interesting or important in a given passage. Where is the melodic line? Which voice does the composer want us to bring out? Here, Chopin has struck, I believe, a rare perfect contrapuntal balance between the hands, asking the performer and listener to fork their attention quite equitably in both directions throughout the prelude. Even most contrapuntal works of Bach ask primarily that our attention dance democratically back and forth between voices (with exceptions, of course), as one voice takes up a subject, or another voice highlights a particularly beautiful counter-motive. But how often is a perfect balance maintained throughout an entire work? Many students of the piano do not spend enough time developing this special skill of divided attention. Use this extraordinary prelude to develop the ability to divide your attention equally in two directions. It is harder to do well than one imagines at first. Of course, the desired musical result is that the two hands sing with equal conviction and compelling beauty.

MM. 1-3 and similar measures: Observe the ties carefully. Be faithful to the "sound picture" Chopin indicates for the second half of these measures.

MM. 5, 6, 7 and similar measures: Notice the prevalence of unusually voiced German augmented sixth chords in this prelude. As we saw in the appendix response to the final question "For Further Exploration" for the previous prelude, augmented sixth chords are considered German if they possess the same four notes as do dominant-seventh chords. They are spelled slightly differently, however, although we have seen that with Chopin that is not always the case. Here he spells them "correctly," but distributes the notes innovatively: the augmented sixth, normally configured in this way is rearranged to form a diminished 10th.

Prelude No. 22: m. 4, beat 2-m. 6

The distribution is quite natural and pianistic, however, and so its originality may be easily overlooked. True innovation often appears camouflaged by the very naturalness - one might say "inevitability"- that is a component of its greatness. One must therefore develop a certain alertness for innovation.

MM. 35-38: In these measures, Chopin omitted the ties analogous with those in the opening measures. I presume that this was an oversight, and have added them in brackets.

Pedaling Possibilities

I recommend the use of pedal to assist the *legato* Chopin implies with the slurs in this prelude. The sound world of this very powerful prelude would also seem to demand greater resonance, and therefore more pedal, than Chopin explicitly indicates. I recommend changing pedal approximately every half bar, carefully holding the notes Chopin ties.

Possible Phrase Structure

1-8 (1-2, 3-4, 5-6, 7-8); 9-16 (9-10, 11-12, 13! 14! 15-16); 17-24 (17-18, 19-20, 21-22, 23-24); 25-34!! (25-26, 27-28, 29-30, 31-32, 33-34); 35-41! (35-36, 37! 38! 39-41)

For Further Exploration

Use mm. 17-23 to develop the alertness for innovation to which I refer above. Chopin here offers a very unusual example of a favored device of his that we have seen frequently throughout the Preludes. Can you determine the device? What makes its use here innovative?

Appendix

Here you will find my responses to the questions posed in "For Further Consideration" for the individual preludes.

It is important to have a score open to the prelude referenced here so that the concepts and discoveries discussed are readily apparent.

PRELUDE NO. 2

One of the more useful questions we can ask of a musical moment is: "What is occurring here for the first time?" When in doubt about what is interesting or beautiful at any moment in a work, try asking that question. Ask that of m. 17 in this prelude. Then ask the same of m. 19, then m. 20. With a little practice, we can find something new about virtually every measure. Every such "event," or novelty, contributes to the story the music tells, and the more conscious we are of these musical events, the more vivid and alive the story.

In m. 17, the left-hand accompaniment figure disappears hauntingly for the first time. In m. 19 Chopin gives the first of several dramatic grand pauses to be found in the *Preludes*. In m. 20 Chopin, the master storyteller, offers—for the first time—only a fragment of the opening theme, as the story winds down. What other first-time events can you find in this prelude?

There are two instances of syncopation in the melodic line in this prelude. Can you find them both? Are they alike or different from each other?

In m. 8, the theme enters on beat three rather than the downbeat, and the first note is shortened to accommodate the unchanged phrase length. But in m. 14, the elongation of the phrase allows the theme to enter in a way that feels "early": the first melodic note occurs on the second beat of the measure and is held through most of the following measure.

PRELUDE NO. 4

What is extraordinary about the first chord in this prelude?

The first chord of the prelude is in first inversion. Note the rarity of this position for a strong opening statement of the tonic chord. Here we see Chopin on the cutting edge of the transition from Classical to Romantic harmonic practice.

What is novel, or significant about the G♯ in m. 8?

The accent on the G# m. 8 may serve to highlight the note's significance in ushering in the return of traditional tonality. See how the chords behave briefly as if we have arrived at the key of A minor. Remember that when we are aware of the significance of an accented note, the accent will be more than a mere accent.

Have you ever spelled a word wrong on test? Is there a chord in this prelude which Chopin may have "misspelled"? What does it mean to misspell a chord?

There is a kind of musical "grammar" concerning the function of notes or chords; music students must practice understanding this grammar just as they must practice their scales. Is there a C7 chord toward the end of this prelude, as Chopin has spelled it? How would a C7 chord normally resolve? To F Major! Does it resolve that way here? No. Another chord containing the same notes as a dominant seventh chord is spelled differently: it is called an augmented sixth chord. In this case the chord should be spelled as an augmented sixth instead of a dominant seventh: the B♭ should be A♯!

The chord as Chopin has spelled it; an inversion of C7:

The chord as Chopin "should" have spelled it; a rearranged augmented 6th:

Here is the chord reconfigured to show the augmented 6th:

It's refreshing, isn't it, that a genius like Chopin may have slipped and forgotten momentarily how a chord's function should determine its spelling! To be fair to Chopin, we should also consider the possibility that he chose to spell the chord with a B♭ because it is easier to read that way. (I have spelled all notes throughout this edition as Chopin did in his manuscript.)

PRELUDE NO. 6

Can you find an extended phrase in the key of the Neapolitan in this prelude? Is the triad itself used in first inversion? Does the phrase lead to the dominant?

The Neapolitan triad in B minor is C major. The phrase that occurs in mm. 11-14 is in C major, and the C major triad occurs in both root position and first inversion. The phrase does lead to the dominant, albeit very smoothly through a brief subdominant and VII diminished 7.

In Prelude No. 4 we saw the raised seventh (i.e. the leading tone) followed closely and expressively by the lowered seventh. Can you find a similar expressive device in this prelude? How does this instance differ from the earlier example?

The expressive occurrence of the raised seventh followed closely by the lowered seventh can be found in mm. 21-22. I believe this poignant juxtaposition is the inspiration for the accent on the final beat of m. 22. In Prelude No. 4, the raised and lowered seventh occur melodically, and the two notes in question are a diminished octave apart. (See the performance note for Prelude No. 4.) In Prelude No. 6, the raised and lowered seventh occur as the upper voice of the accompanying chords, and are a half step apart.

PRELUDE NO. 7

This prelude offers an opportunity to develop an important aspect of musical insight: the capacity to see something new in comparable phrases. The performer who remains conscious of these nuances throughout the piece will communicate them to the listener, who will be aware of them as elements of an unfolding story. In each of the eight phrase segments, determine what is happening for the first time.

Often there are several new elements or events in a given phrase or phrase segment, and composers frequently use simultaneous innovations to highlight a musical moment's importance. Here are some examples of new events in each of the phrase segments 2-8 of Prelude No. 7. These are by no means exhaustive; see if you can find further examples.

In segment 2 Chopin includes a second voice in the right hand. The resulting thirds impart an Italianate flavor to the prelude, and this prelude, which is also a mazurka, begins to feel like a miniature barcarolle as well.

Prelude No. 7: mm. 2-4

Chopin adds a voice.

In segment 3 Chopin ties a note to the repeated chords for the first time, adding a delicious ninth to the dominant harmony, and also changes the right-hand harmonic interval from thirds to sixths. This movement from thirds to sixths also adds to the barcarolle feel.

Prelude No. 7: mm. 4-6

In segment 4 Chopin repeats the anacrusis (or pickup) on the downbeat for the first time. The effect of this repetition is unexpectedly tender.

Prelude No. 7: mm. 6-8

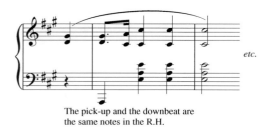

The pick-up and the downbeat are the same notes in the R.H.

In segment 5 he ties the pickup to the downbeat, to which he adds a third voice for an even richer texture. The resulting chord is also a *barcarolle* favorite, a version of V13.

Prelude No. 7: mm. 8-10

Chopin adds a third voice on the downbeat.

Notice that all segments thus far include repeated chords. In segment 6 Chopin finally changes the chord on the second downbeat of the segment, i.e. the last of the three chords.

Prelude No. 7: mm. 10-12

There is a change in the repeated chords for the first time (on the downbeat of m. 12).

This is the most expressive event thus far. It is also the first departure from tonic and dominant harmony.

Here Chopin brings together several innovations to heighten the significance of this special moment. In segment 7 Chopin takes the principle of change in the repeated chords even further: Now there is change on the second and the third chords (not just the third), and the change is in an inner voice while the upper voice remains unchanged. This is an event of great beauty, resulting in an exquisite V9 chord.

Prelude No. 7: mm. 12-14

There is a change on *each* of the repeated chords, but the upper voice remains the same.

In segment 8 Chopin includes the first ornament of the prelude, a single grace note. But there is another more interesting novelty. The dotted rhythm has always, until now, involved an ascending second. Here, in the final segment, the dotted rhythm finally involves a descending second. This adds to the experience of closure conveyed by this final segment.

Prelude No. 7: mm. 14-16

The dotted rhythm is now a *descending* second:

The grace note is new.

Did Chopin consciously fashion each of these new events and permutations for every segment? Of course, we cannot know for sure—certainly "yes" for some; probably not for all. Chopin was a master storyteller: in all likelihood his extraordinarily natural creative gift simply led him to vary the phrases spontaneously throughout the unfolding story. Notice how alive the prelude is at all times, even though the rhythm is identical in all eight segments.

PRELUDE NO. 9

Chopin was a master of harmonic innovation and experimentation. There are two very interesting harmonic approaches to the dominant in this prelude. Can you find them both?

In m. 8 Chopin reaches the major mediant (enharmonically spelled as A♭ major). This is a harmonic event that he enjoys frequently. Look for examples of it in the *Polonaise, Op. 53,* (see the very last few measures), the *Etude, Op. 10, No. 1,* (just before the "recap") and a very interesting variant of it in Prelude No. 8 (see mm. 18-19). But notice here in Prelude No. 9 that the major mediant "melts" briefly into the minor—and therefore more "normal"—mediant of G♯ minor, before moving to the dominant and then home to E major. Thus, in this case Chopin takes the "edge" off of the progression from the major mediant through the dominant to the home key. But Chopin tries out a thoroughly original—and quite edgy—take on the progression at m. 11, moving directly from the lowered major mediant of G major to the dominant B major in the final cadence.

How might you attempt to tell the rhythmic story of this prelude in words? It might start out with a rhythmic disagreement between the hands. Where would it go from there?

After the initial "disagreement" between the hands, the rhythmic story might entail the gradual "convincing" of one hand by the other, with agreement being reached only at the very last V-I cadence. Take note that only in this final cadence do the hands play the 32nd notes simultaneously. This lends the final cadence an air of triumph.

PRELUDE NO. 15

Chopin seems to have set himself a compositional challenge, in the form of a limit, in this prelude. What is that challenge? Put another way, he adopted the musical equivalent of a poet's rhyme scheme. What is that scheme?

With the repetition of the A♭/G♯ through much of this prelude, Chopin limits the amount of harmonic creativity available to him. Considering how richly varied he usually prefers his harmonic palette, we may marvel at the embrace of limitation here, and the enormously satisfying result. This embrace is not unlike the decision of a poet to utilize a rhyme scheme, and thus limit the words at his disposal. Of course, Chopin does depart occasionally from his "rhyme" scheme (as poets often do as well), and also repeats pitches other than A♭/G♯ in this prelude. Look closely at the repeated pitches throughout the prelude. Does he ever repeat a pitch other than the fifth degree of the key of the moment? (Consider, for example, the brief excursion into A♭ minor on the first page. How is the repetition of the A♭ in these measures different from the repetition of the same pitch while in the key of D♭?)

PRELUDE NO. 20

As Thomas Higgins points out in his "Notes Toward a Performance" of the Preludes, Chopin rather humorously adds a note in the manuscript implying that it was on the advice of a certain "Monsieur xxx who is often right" that he repeats the second phrase. How does this repetition leave the piece with an unusual structure?

If Chopin's original impulse had been to state the second phrase only a single time it would have left the prelude entirely "square," with two four-bar phrases consisting solely of measures of identical four-beat rhythm (plus the final measure with a single chord). With the repetition of the second phrase Chopin introduces a deeply satisfying "curve," a third four-bar phrase without a fourth. Try playing the prelude without repeating the second phrase. Note how fleeting the effect is when the lovely second phrase occurs only once.

PRELUDE NO. 22

Use mm. 17-23 to develop your eye for innovation. Chopin here offers a very unusual example of a favored device of his that we have seen frequently throughout the Preludes. Can you determine the device? What makes its use here innovative?

MM. 17-22 appear at a glance to be centered on the key of D♭ major, until we realize that the G in these measures is always natural rather than flat. With G♮ the key is not D♭, but A♭ major. This is easy to miss because the A♭ chord itself makes only brief appearances in the phrase. What significance does A♭ major carry in the key of G minor? Yes, this is an extraordinary occurrence of the Neapolitan key of A♭, revolving—with striking effect—around its subdominant, D♭.

—Brian Ganz

Prelude in A Minor

Frédéric Chopin
Op. 28, No. 2

Prelude in E Minor

Frédéric Chopin
Op. 28, No. 4

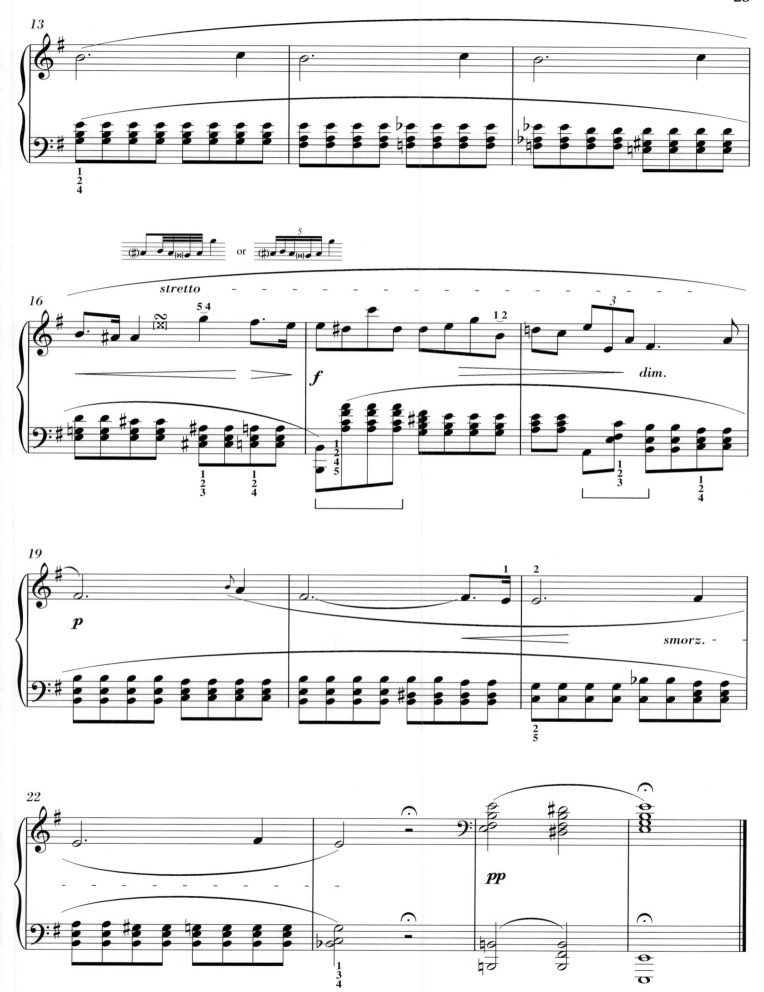

Prelude in B Minor

Frédéric Chopin
Op. 28, No. 6

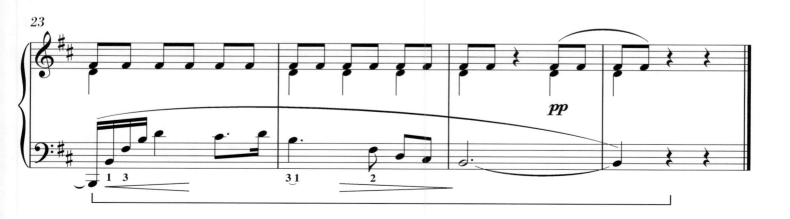

Prelude in A Major

Frédéric Chopin
Op. 28, No. 7

Prelude in E Major

Frédéric Chopin
Op. 28, No. 9

* *We have followed the first-edition notation for this prelude by offsetting the 16th note in this rhythmic figure throughout. However, Chopin's manuscript presents the figure thus:*

If the manuscript version is adopted in performance, all 16ths should be played simultaneously with the final eighth of the lower-voice triplet.

* *If the manuscript version is adopted, beat 1, m. 8 should be played thus:*

See performance notes p. 11 for further discussion of this issue.

Prelude in D-flat Major

Frédéric Chopin
Op. 28, No. 15

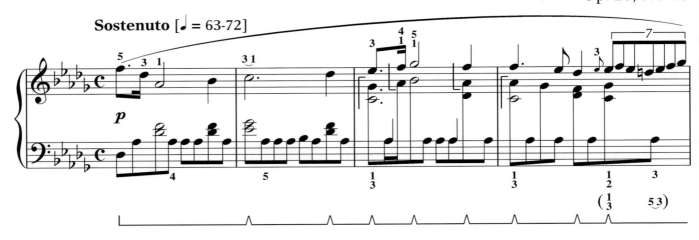

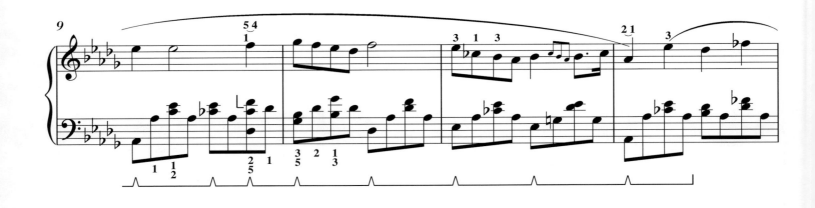

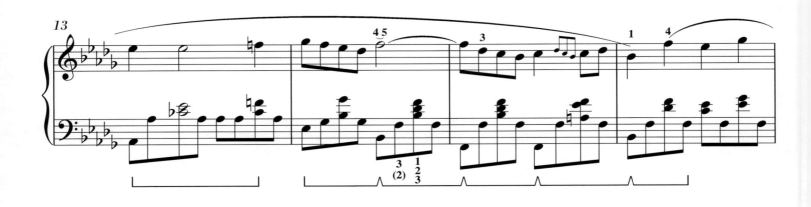

Prelude in C Minor

Frédéric Chopin
Op. 28, No. 20

Prelude in G Minor

Frédéric Chopin
Op. 28, No. 22

Molto agitato [♩. = 132-144]

ABOUT THE EDITOR

BRIAN GANZ

Brian Ganz is widely regarded as one of the leading pianists of his generation. After he performed the Preludes in an all-Chopin recital in Washington D.C., the Washington Post declared, "One comes away from a recital by pianist Brian Ganz not only exhilarated by the power of the performance but also moved by his search for artistic truth."

Mr. Ganz was winner of one of two First Grand Prizes awarded in the 1989 Marguerite Long-Jacques Thibaud International Piano Competition in Paris. That same year, he won a Beethoven Fellowship awarded by the American Pianists Association, and in 1991 he was a silver medalist with third prize in the Queen Elisabeth of Belgium International Piano Competition. After his performance in the finals of the Brussels competition, the critic for La Libre Belgique wrote, "We don't have the words to speak of this fabulous musician who lives music with a generous urgency and brings his public into a state of intense joy."

He has appeared as soloist with such orchestras as the St. Louis Symphony, the St. Petersburg (Russia) Philharmonic, the City of London Sinfonia, L'Orchestre Lamoureux, and L'Orchestre Philharmonique de Monte Carlo, and has performed under the baton of such conductors as Leonard Slatkin, Mstislav Rostropovich, and Pinchas Zukerman. He made his recording debut in 1992 for the Gailly label in Belgium, and his recordings of Chopin and Dutilleux have been released on the Accord label in Paris. In 2001, he began a project with Maestoso Records in which he will record the complete works of Chopin.

Mr. Ganz is a graduate of the Peabody Conservatory of Music, where he studied with Leon Fleisher. Earlier teachers include Ylda Novik and the late Claire Deene. Gifted as a teacher himself, Mr. Ganz is Artist-in-Residence at St. Mary's College of Maryland, where he has been a member of the piano faculty since 1986. In 2000, he joined the piano faculty of the Peabody Conservatory.